Here Is My Heart

LOVE POEMS

Compiled by William Jay Smith

Illustrated by Jane Dyer

Little, Brown and Company

Boston   New York   Toronto   London

First Edition

Copyright acknowledgments appear on page 50.

Library of Congress Cataloging-in-Publication Data
Here is my heart : love poems / compiled by William Jay Smith ;
illustrated by Jane Dyer. — 1st edition
      p.   cm.
Includes index.
ISBN 0-316-19765-3
I. Love poetry, English. 2. Love poetry, American. I. Smith, William Jay.
II. Dyer, Jane.
PR1184.H4 1999
821.008'03543 — dc21   97-26665

10 9 8 7 6 5 4 3 2 1

TWP

Published simultaneously in Canada by Little, Brown & Company (Canada) Limited

Printed in Singapore

The illustrations for this book were done in Caran D'Ache colored pencils on Arches 140 lb. hot press paper.
The text was set in Centaur. The display lines were set in Ovidius Demi.

Very fine is my valentine.
Very fine and very mine.

Very mine is my valentine very mine and very fine.
Very fine is my valentine and mine, very fine
          very mine and mine is my valentine.

— Gertrude Stein

CONTENTS

A VALENTINE

Oh, little loveliest lady mine,
What shall I send for your valentine?
Buds are asleep and blossoms are dead,
And the snow beats down on my poor little head:
So, little loveliest lady mine,
Here is my heart for your valentine.

—*Laura E. Richards*

A VALENTINE

Frost flowers on the window glass,
Hopping chickadees that pass,
Bare old elms that bend and sway,
Pussy willows, soft and gray,

Silver clouds across the sky,
Lacy snowflakes flitting by,
Icicles like fringe in line —
That is Outdoor's valentine!

—*Eleanor Hammond*

Tomorrow is Saint Valentine's day,
All in the morning betime,
And I a maid at your window
To be your Valentine.

— *William Shakespeare*

LOVE ME LITTLE, LOVE ME LONG

You say to me that your affection's strong;
Pray love me little, so you love me long.

— *Robert Herrick*

4

CRESCENT MOON

And Dick said, "Look what I have found!"
And when we saw we danced around,
And made our feet just tip the ground.

We skipped our toes and sang, "Oh-lo.
Oh-who, oh-who, oh what do you know!
Oh-who, oh-hi, oh-loo, kee-lo!"

We clapped our hands and sang, "Oh-ee!"
It made us jump and laugh to see
The little new moon above the tree.

— *Elizabeth Madox Roberts*

HERE'S TO ONE

Here's to one and only one,
    And may that one be he
Who loves but one and only one,
    And may that one be me.

— Anonymous

THE CANAL BANK

I know a girl,
    And a girl knows me,
    And the owl says, what!
    And the owl says, who?

But what we know
    We both agree
    That nobody else
    Shall hear or see;

It's all between herself and me:
    To wit? said the owl,
    To woo! said I,
    To-what! To-wit! To-woo!

— James Stephens

VALENTINE

Chipmunks jump, and
Greensnakes slither.
Rather burst than
Not be with her.

Bluebirds fight, but
Bears are stronger.
We've got fifty
Years or longer.

Hoptoads hop, but
Hogs are fatter.
Nothing else but
Us can matter.

— *Donald Hall*

NOTES

Butterfly trembles when the wind blows.
You walk near me.
The dog barks at the loud moon.
When you come to me,
I speak softly, softly,
Until we are silent together.
For two hundred years
This pine tree has been trained to grow sideways.
I have known you only one week,
But I bend as you walk toward me.

— Paul Engle

MY VALENTINE

I will make you brooches
And toys for your delight
Of bird song at morning
And starshine at night.
I will build a palace
Fit for you and me,

      Of green days in forests
      And blue days at sea.

— *Robert Louis Stevenson*

I LOVE YOU MORE
THAN APPLESAUCE

I love you more than applesauce,
than peaches and a plum,
than chocolate hearts and cherry tarts
and berry bubblegum.

I love you more than lemonade
and seven-layer cakes,
than lollipops and candy drops
and thick vanilla shakes.

I love you more than marzipan,
than marmalade on toast,
oh I love pies of any size,
but I love YOU the most.

— *Jack Prelutsky*

CHINESE VALENTINE

They say
it is bad luck
to cut a long green bean.
I give you this bean, like my love—
whole, fresh.

— *Janet Wong*

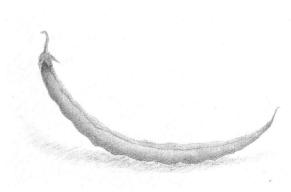

SONG FOR THE MOON

I've done my duties,
   done my chores:

I've lighted the stars
   and scrubbed the floors
and polished the silver
   and waxed the moon—

so we can go dancing
   sooner than soon!

— *Michael Stillman*

GIVE ME MY ROMEO

Give me my Romeo and when he shall die,
Take him and cut him out in little stars,
And he will make the face of heaven so fine
That all the world will be in love with night
And pay no worship to the garish sun.

—*William Shakespeare*

LOVE SONG

Cold star hangs
In the sycamore tree,
Day go night,
Night go day,
Summer come early,
Seed come thick,
Frost on the barley,
Kiss me quick!

—*Julia Randall*

RETURNING THE RED GLOVES

I am returning
the red
gloves
you left in Vera's
pocket

They are soft shells
that miss
the snails that would give them
their own slow
speed

They are five-room houses
waiting for their inhabitants
to come home

They are red wings
that have forgotten
how to fly

When you receive them
put them on

for like lovers who warm each other
all night
you will warm them
and they will warm
your hands

which must be
lost
Valentines
without
their envelopes

— *Siv Cedering*

COCK ROBIN

Cock Robin got up early
    At the break of day
And went to Jenny's window
    To sing a roundelay.

He sang Cock Robin's love
    To the pretty Jenny Wren
And when he got unto the end
    Then he began again.

— Old Rhyme

OLD WOMAN, OLD WOMAN

Old woman, old woman, shall we go a-shearing?
Speak a little louder, sir; I'm very thick of hearing.

Old woman, old woman, shall we go a-gleaning?
Speak a little louder, sir; I cannot tell your meaning.

Old woman, old woman, shall we go a-walking?
Speak a little louder, sir; or what's the use of talking?

Old woman, old woman, shall I kiss you dearly?
Thank you, kind sir, I hear you very clearly.

— Old Rhyme   15

THE WALTZER IN THE HOUSE

A sweet, a delicate white mouse,
   A little blossom of a beast,
   Is waltzing in the house
   Among the crackers and the yeast.

O the swaying of his legs!
O the bobbing of his head!
The lady, beautiful and kind,
The blue-eyed mistress, lately wed,
Has almost laughed away her wits
To see the pretty mouse that sits
On his tiny pink behind
And swaying, bobbing, begs.

She feeds him tarts and curds,
Seed packaged for the birds,
And figs, and nuts, and cheese;
Polite as Pompadour to please
The dainty waltzer of her house,
The sweet, the delicate, the innocent white mouse.

As in a dream, as in a trance,
She loves his rhythmic elegance,
She laughs to see his bobbing dance.

— *Stanley Kunitz*

ROSES ARE RED

Roses are red,
Violets are blue;
The stars have the heavens
But I have you.

Roses are red,
Lilacs are mauve;
You keep me sizzling
Like a hot kitchen stove.

Roses are red,
Pinks are pink;
If I had a love potion
I'd ask you to drink.

— William Jay Smith

VALENTINE VERSES

I'll be yours, sweet cricket,
Till the sun freezes over
And the desert is flooded
And covered with clover;
Till it snows in the tropics
And camels wear socks;
And grandfather wristwatches
Are grandfather clocks.

— *William Jay Smith*

THE ROSE FAMILY

The rose is a rose,
And was always a rose,
But the theory now goes
That the apple's a rose,
And the pear is, and so's
The plum, I suppose.
The dear only knows
What will next prove a rose.
You, of course, are a rose—
But were always a rose.

— *Robert Frost*

A GIFT OF ROSES

I wanted this morning to bring you a gift of roses;
But I took so many in my wide belt,
The tightened knots could not contain them all,

And burst asunder. The roses, taking wing
On the wind, were all blown out to sea,
Following the water, never to return;

The waves were red with them as if aflame.
This evening my dress bears their perfume still:
You may take from it now their fragrant souvenir.

— Marceline Desbordes-Valmore
Translated from the French by Barbara Howes

PERMANENTLY

One day the Nouns were clustered in the street.
An Adjective walked by, with her dark beauty.
The Nouns were struck, moved, changed.
The next day a Verb drove up, and created the Sentence.

Each Sentence says one thing—for example, "Although it
    was a dark rainy day when the Adjective walked by, I
    shall remember the pure and sweet expression on her face
    until the day I perish from the green, effective earth."
Or, "Will you please close the window, Andrew?"
Or, for example, "Thank you, the pink pot of flowers on
    the window sill has changed color recently to a light
    yellow, due to the heat from the boiler factory which
    exists nearby."

In the springtime the Sentences and the Nouns lay silently
    on the grass.
A lonely Conjunction here and there would call, "And!
    But!"
But the Adjective did not emerge.

As the adjective is lost in the sentence,
So I am lost in your eyes, ears, nose, and throat —
You have enchanted me with a single kiss
Which can never be undone
Until the destruction of language.

— *Kenneth Koch*

PENNY CANDY

Penny candy
Sugar hearts
Oranges &
Lemon tarts

Ask me where my
Money goes?
To buy my sweetheart
Fancy clothes.

— *Clyde Watson*

LOVE

Love is an apple, round and firm,
without a blemish or a worm.
Bite into it and you will find
you've found your heart and lost your mind.

— *Brooke Astor*

IF APPLES WERE PEARS

If apples were pears,
And peaches were plums,
And the rose had a different name,
If tigers were bears,
And fingers were thumbs,
I'd love you just the same!

— *Old Rhyme*

I LOVE YOU LITTLE

I love you little,
I love you lots,
My love for you would fill ten pots,
Fifteen buckets,
Sixteen cans,
Three teacups,
And four dishpans.

— *Old Rhyme*   25

UNICORN

The Unicorn with the long white horn
   Is beautiful and wild.
He gallops across the forest green
So quickly that he's seldom seen
Where Peacocks their blue feathers preen
   And strawberries grow wild.
He flees the hunter and the hounds,
Upon black earth his white hoof pounds,
Over cold mountain streams he bounds
   And comes to a meadow mild;
There, when he kneels to take his nap,
He lays his head in a lady's lap
   As gently as a child.

—*William Jay Smith*

IN THIS PICTURE

In this picture
I sketch a forest
in the afternoon,

white pines overhead,
leaves crunching
under my feet.

I am walking
looking for you
everywhere,

along the trail,
waiting in the meadow
or at the big rock,

but wherever I go
up or down
you are hidden,

so I step out
of the picture
and draw you

waiting by
Bullfrog Quarry
just as I come up the trail.

You are surprised
that I have been
looking for you

and thank me
for putting you
into my picture

and on you hike
as I sketch myself
following closely behind.

— *Myra Cohn Livingston*

INVITATION

You who have meant to come, come now
With strangeness on the morning snow
Before the early morning plow
Makes half the snowy strangeness go.

You who have meant to come, come now
When only *your* footprints will show,
Before one overburdened bough
Spills snow above on snow below.

You who were meant to come, come now.
If you were meant to come, you'll know.

— *Robert Francis*

30

GIVE ME ONE KISS

Give me one kiss
    And no more;
If so be, this
    Makes you poor;
To enrich you,
    I'll restore
For that one, two
    Thousand more.

— *Robert Herrick*

FOR YOU

Here is a building
I have built for you.
The bricks are butter yellow.
Every window shines.
And at each an orange cat is curled,
lulled by the summer sun.
The door invites you in.
The mat is warm.
Inside there is a chair
so soft and blue
the pillows look like sky.
In all the world
no one but you
may sit in that cloud chair.
I'll sit near by.

— *Karla Kuskin*

BLISS

Let me fetch sticks,
Let me fetch stones,
Throw me your bones,
Teach me your tricks.

When you go ride,
Let me go run,
You in the sun,
Me at your side;

When you go swim,
Let me go too
Both lost in blue
Up to the brim;

Let me do this,
Let me do that—
What you are at,
That is my bliss.

— *Eleanor Farjeon*

BLACK GIRL

Yes, she is black. Her cheek has no rose tint,
No burst of gold like grain against the sky.
Coal, too, is black. But light a match to it,
And into flaming roses it leaps high.

— *Paul-Jean Toulet*
Translated from the French by William Jay Smith

JUKE BOX LOVE SONG

I could take the Harlem night
and wrap around you,
Take the neon lights and make a crown,
Take the Lenox Avenue buses,
Taxis, subways,
And for your love song tone their rumble down.
Take Harlem's heartbeat,
Make a drumbeat,
Put it on a record, let it whirl,
And while we listen to it play,
Dance with you till day—
Dance with you, my sweet brown Harlem girl.

— Langston Hughes

SONG

LIZARDS' RING
(not actual size)

The he-lizard is crying.
The she-lizard is crying.

The he-lizard and the she-lizard
with little white aprons

Have lost without wanting to
their wedding ring.

Ah, their little leaden wedding ring,
ah, their little ring of lead!

A large sky without people
carries the birds in its balloon.

The sun, rotund captain,
wears a satin waistcoat.

Look how old they are!
How old the lizards are!

Oh! how they cry and cry,
Oh! Oh! How they go on crying!

— *Federico García Lorca*
Translated from the Spanish
by Stephen Spender and J. L. Gili

A PAVANE FOR THE NURSERY

Now touch the air softly,
Step gently. One, two . . .
I'll love you till roses
Are robin's-egg blue;
I'll love you till gravel
Is eaten for bread,
And lemons are orange,
And lavender's red.

Now touch the air softly,
Swing gently the broom.
I'll love you till windows
Are all of a room;
And the table is laid,
And the table is bare,
And the ceiling reposes
On bottomless air.

I'll love you till Heaven
Rips the stars from his coat,
And the Moon rows away in
A glass-bottomed boat;
And Orion steps down
Like a diver below,
And Earth is ablaze,
And Ocean aglow.

So touch the air softly,
And swing the broom high.
We will dust the gray mountains,
And sweep the blue sky;
And I'll love you as long
As the furrow the plow,
As However is Ever,
And Ever is Now.

— William Jay Smith

39

THE MARMALADE MAN MAKES A DANCE TO MEND US

Tiger, sunflowers, King of Cats,
Cow and rabbit, mend your ways.
I the needle, you the thread —
follow me through mist and maze.

Fox and hound, go paw in paw.
Cat and rat, be best of friends.
Lamb and tiger, walk together
Dancing starts where fighting ends.

— *Nancy Willard*

THE NEEDLE'S EYE

The needle's eye it doth supply the thread that runs so true,
There's many a beau that I've let go because I wanted you,
You, oh, you, because I wanted you.

The needle's eye, it doth combine the threads you love so true,
Many a beau have I let go because I wanted you,
You, oh, you, because I wanted you.

—*American Folk Song*

SWEET AS A PICKLE
AND CLEAN AS A PIG

When you're sweet as a pickle
And clean as a pig—
I'll give you a nickel
And dance you a jig.

— *Carson McCullers*

BINGO! BANGO!

There'd be an orchestra
    Bingo! Bango!
Playing for us
    To dance the tango,
And people would clap
    When we arose,
At her sweet face
    And my new clothes.

— *F. Scott Fitzgerald*

THE QUEEN OF THE NILE

Said the Queen of the Nile
  By the green palm tree:
   "It is Our desire
    That you come to tea
     Thursday at twenty-three
     Past three
      Under the Royal Canopy
      In Our Golden Barge
      On the River Nile
       Beside the Mediterranean
       Sea."

I bowed, and said:
  "Most certainly!"
   To the Queen of the Nile
    By the green palm tree.

—*William Jay Smith*

LOVE LYRIC

Nothing, nothing can keep me from my love
Standing on the other shore.

Not even old crocodile
There on the sandbank between us
Can keep us apart.

I go in spite of him,
I walk upon the waves,
Her love flows back across the water,
Turning waves to solid earth
For me to walk on.

The river is our Enchanted Sea.

— Anonymous
Translated from the ancient Egyptian by Noel Stock

THE OUTRIGGER CANOE

If I had a boat—
   If right now
      Someone would bring me
         Out of the blue
            The boat that I wanted—
           An outrigger canoe—

      Do you know what I'd do?

I would paddle around
   Where the big waves pound
      Until I found
   The place where you
      Out in the blue
Lived on an island green and fine
Covered all over with moonflower vine
   And I would say, "Will you be mine?"

And you would say, "Yes, I will if you
   Take me in your outrigger canoe!"

So together we'd paddle off through the blue
   Around the island green and fine.

The moon would come up and the stars would shine . . .
   I would be yours,
      And you would be mine

      If I had a boat!

—*William Jay Smith*

INDEX